RISING

BY JOHN BRADSHAW

IT IS WRITTEN
INTERNATIONAL

&

Pacific Press Publishing Association

Art Direction & Layout by

GUILDHOUSE GROUP

Cover Design by

PALMER HALVORSON

Text Typeset:

ADOBE GARAMOND PRO

Most Bible texts taken from the King James Version and
New King James Version, copyright 1979, 1980, 1982 by
Thomas Nelson, Inc. Used by permission.
Printed in the United States of America
by Pacific Press Publishing Association
Nampa, Idaho / Oshawa, Ontario, Canada
www.pacificpress.com

ISBN: 978-1-937173-00-5

CONTENTS

Babylon Rising 5

Characteristics of Babylon 13

Where There's Smoke... 21

Conspiracy 35

Who Is Babylon? 51

The Writing on the Wall 59

The Final Call 69

History's Greatest Event 79

Chapter One

BABYLON RISING

It was an interesting thing for a journalist to say. At any other time, the statement might have been entirely appropriate. But just after an enormous earthquake had struck northeastern Japan in March 2011, and it was evident that this was going to be a massive disaster of the worst kind, the timing of the comment seemed—to me at least—to be a little awry.

Measuring 9.0 on the Richter scale—the largest in Japan's history—the earthquake caused catastrophic damage, and the ensuing tsunami wiped away entire communities. Journalists reported live as the angry floodwaters deluged cities and claimed thousands of lives.

As my wife, Melissa, and I were gazing at our computer screen in bewilderment, a journalist noted with consolation in his voice that of all the nations in the world, Japan was "perhaps the best equipped to deal with the challenges presented by an earthquake."

No doubt the intention of the journalist's words was to communicate the fact that buildings in Japan are well engineered, to deal with the shock of a serious earthquake. Coming from New Zealand—a country that is no stranger to seismic activity, and which suffered its own devastating temblor just a few weeks before the Japanese event—I'm well aware of the necessity of having buildings in earthquake zones constructed according to the strictest codes and highest standards.

Not only is Japan equipped with tsunami sirens, which alert people to hurry to high ground, but the people of Japan are well educated regarding what to do should an earthquake or tsunami strike. Japan could indeed be described as well equipped to deal with an earthquake.

But the thing about earthquakes is that, as *Newsweek* magazine reported, "all geologic events are sudden, and all are unexpected if not necessarily entirely unanticipated." ["The Scariest Earthquake Is Yet to Come," *Newsweek*, March 13, 2011.]

In other words, you can prepare for an earthquake, but you can't really *prepare* for an earthquake. They're not like the 1 p.m. train from Central Station. You really don't know when they're going to come, and when they do, you really don't know what you're going to get.

Tsunamis are the same—nobody knows just when a tsunami might initially strike, and once you get the warning that one is on its way, there's only so much you can do.

As *Newsweek* reported in the same article, "in this corner of northeast Japan, with its wide plains of rice meadows and ideal factory sites and conveniently flat airport locations, there may well be a great deal of inland—but there is almost no uphill."

Many people had only 30 seconds to evade the incoming tide. In stunned silence, Melissa and I watched video footage of the maddened torrent sweeping away vehicles and buildings, with people desperately fleeing from the raging floodwaters.

As prepared as Japan might have been, its extensive preparations were not enough to avoid the incredible devastation caused by the earthquake and tsunami, as well as the damage to the nuclear power station. This brought fear, panic and confusion to the entire nation and beyond.

For a number of countries in the world, living with the specter of the next "big one" constantly looming is a fact of everyday life. These countries know that when it comes to earthquakes, it is not a matter of *if* they will strike, but *when*, and of how much damage will be done and how many lives will be lost.

But you can't ever tell how bad an earthquake will be. You can be fairly sure an earthquake will be bad, and that it could be very bad. It could even be utterly devastating. However, there's no way of knowing how bad the bad thing is going to be until the bad thing arrives.

In the Bible, God warns planet Earth that the "Big One" is coming. The book of Daniel speaks of a coming "time of trouble such as never was" (Daniel 12:1).

Like a predicted earthquake, it is difficult to appreciate what this time of trouble is really going to be like. In a time of uncertainty on planet Earth, with wars being fought and economies straining, the Bible suggests that the worst is yet to come.

The Bible itself illuminates the matter in Daniel's companion book, the book of Revelation. The Apostle John wrote Revelation from the Island of Patmos. Located in the Aegean Sea, Patmos is now a Greek island, though it is located much closer to Turkey than Greece.

In the last century, Patmos has been the domain of not only Greece but of Italy and Nazi Germany. When John was there, it was governed by the Roman Empire. John was a prisoner of Rome due to his faith in Jesus Christ.

No stranger to trouble, John wrote the book of Revelation to show God's people "things which must shortly come to pass" (Revelation 1:1) in large part because Jesus would "come quickly" (Revelation 22:10).

The title of the book of Revelation is derived from the Greek word *apokalupsis* (from which is derived the word "apocalypse"), and means "an unveiling". That is, the book of Revelation is a revelation—or an unveiling—of the future history of planet Earth, and of God's dealings with the world during that time.

Revelation presents God as a God of love. "And the Spirit and the bride say, Come. And let him that heareth say, Come. And let him that is athirst come. And whosoever will, let him take the water of life freely" (Revelation 22:17).

The book of Revelation reveals Jesus as a gracious, merciful Savior, soon to return to this Earth and ransom His people. "Unto Him that loved us, and washed us from our sins in His own blood...behold, He cometh with clouds; and every eye shall see Him" (Revelation 1:5, 7).

At the same time, God's last-day book of the Bible instructs people as to how they should live while preparing for Christ's return. "Fear God and give glory to Him, for the hour of His judgment is come, and worship Him who made heaven, and earth, and the sea, and the fountains of waters" (Revelation 14:7). God's waiting people, along with having faith in Him, will worship God as Creator.

The book of Revelation also warns God's people about the very real and severe spiritual dangers that will confront the world down through history, as those with tremendous power turn against the people of God in the time immediately prior to Jesus' return.

Revelation chronicles a future time when an authoritarian power will emerge and bear almost universal sway over the people of the world, to the extent that those who refuse to cooperate with its agenda for the world will face the loss of their lives. "And he had power to give life unto the image of the beast, that the image of the beast should both speak, and cause that as many as would not worship the image of the beast should be killed" (Revelation 13:15).

John wrote that this "beast" would have profound power and influence. The nations of the world will be subservient to this beast, it will govern the world's economy (Revelation 18:3), and it will rule in the area of personal finance to such an extent that it will prevent many people from being able to buy and sell (Revelation 13:17).

Remarkably, John says this power will go so far as to strip away freedom of conscience, even to the point of regulating how people may worship God (Revelation 13:8, 15).

The Bible refers to this entity in various ways. Daniel called it the "Little Horn" (Daniel 7:8). The Apostle Paul called it the "man of sin" (2 Thessalonians 2:3). And John in Revelation referred to it as both "the beast" and "Babylon".

Not only does John refer to Babylon in four chapters of the book of Revelation, but he also devotes two entire chapters of Revelation to discussing Babylon: who it is, where it is, what it is like, and ultimately, the circumstances surrounding its downfall.

John states clearly that this Babylon has a profound—and spiritually deadly—effect on the world in the days preceding the return of Jesus.

In the first few verses of Revelation chapter 17, John states that there is a time coming when Babylon will have a massive influence over the people of the entire world. Virtually controlling the rulers of the world, she will unite her power with that of world governments, enjoy phenomenal wealth, blaspheme against God and persecute the followers of God.

I can imagine someone reading this and saying, "Really?" If the Bible is to be believed, then the answer is, "Yes, really." It isn't a question of *if*—it's a question of *when*. And as with the 2011 earthquake that moved the Japanese island of Honshu eight feet to the east, when it comes, it is going to be *big*.

When can this be expected to take place? Without trying to set a date for this, we can know for sure—based on some of the plainest statements in the Bible and the corroborating evidence we see in the world around us—that Jesus is coming back soon.

The signs of His coming, as enumerated in Matthew 24 and Luke 21, are being fulfilled even as you read this book. And before Jesus returns to this earth, the unfulfilled chapters of the book of Revelation will have to be fulfilled. Which means the prophecies regarding Babylon are soon to unfold before us.

Here's what Revelation makes abundantly clear: something called Babylon is going to ride roughshod over the entire planet. There will be massive persecution, liberty of conscience will be forfeited, religious freedom is going to disappear, the world's economies will be gripped in a brutal stranglehold, and the world's governments will fall at Babylon's feet—all before Jesus returns. Which is to say—soon.

This leads us to only one conclusion: while we go about our lives, "eating and drinking, marrying and giving in marriage" (Matthew 24:38), while we work and play and eat and sleep—whether we understand it or not, and as unable as we are to truly understand just how serious this will be—surely, steadily and stealthily...Babylon is rising.

Chapter Two

CHARACTERISTICS OF BABYLON

In 1860, French explorer Henri Mouhot located the ruins of a magnificent ancient city. Virtually unknown to the outside world, the abandoned city of Angkor, in the heart of Cambodia, would soon fascinate people everywhere. More than 500 years after its inhabitants fled this immense city, its 1,000+ temples—covering more ground than modern Paris and containing more stone than the pyramids of Egypt—raised some intriguing questions.

Who were the builders of this mysterious city, and why did they flee? Today, many questions about Angkor have been answered, and the city—home to Angkor Wat, possibly the world's largest single religious monument—attracts hundreds of thousands of visitors each year. Once shrouded in intrigue, Angkor is now a UNESCO World Heritage Site.

In the book of Revelation, the Bible speaks of a mysterious city that would captivate the attention of the world in the latter days of earth's history. This Babylon shares its name with the ancient city that headquartered the dominant kingdom of its age.

After a splendid reign of unimaginable power and wealth, Babylon of old was destroyed, with God declaring that ancient Babylon would never again be inhabited.

"And Babylon, the glory of kingdoms, the beauty of the Chaldees' excellency, shall be as when God overthrew Sodom and Gomorrah. It shall never be inhabited, neither shall it be dwelt in from generation to generation: neither shall the Arabian pitch tent there; neither shall the shepherds make their fold there" (Isaiah 13:19, 20).

But in spite of that proclamation, Babylon is back in the New Testament. Revelation 17:18 describes Babylon as a "great city, which reigneth over the kings of the earth," while Revelation 18:16 speaks of "that great city, that was clothed in fine linen, and purple, and scarlet, and decked with gold, and precious stones and pearls."

Chapters 17 and 18 of the book of Revelation deal exclusively with the city of Babylon, and the description given of Babylon is often far from flattering.

In Revelation 17, Babylon is described as a "great whore" that intoxicates the people of the world and is involved in illicit alliances with the governments of the world. Babylon is called "the mother of harlots" and is described as being drunk "with the blood of the martyrs of Jesus."

In order for us to understand who the "last-days Babylon" is and how it is going to rise to power, it is essential that we first go back in time and learn something about the Babylon of Old Testament times. The book of Revelation draws from the Old Testament for its images and symbols. As we study the original Babylon, we'll discover the characteristics of the last-days entity ancient Babylon prefigured.

The historical kingdom of Babylonia was situated in what was known as the "fertile crescent", stretching south to the Persian Gulf and, ultimately, west to the Mediterranean Sea.

The Tigris and Euphrates rivers ran through the kingdom, which today would lie largely in what we now know as modern-day Iraq. The city of Babylon was the capital of Babylonia, famous for the Hanging Gardens of Babylon, one of the seven wonders of the ancient world, built by King Nebuchadnezzar for his homesick wife.

The historian Herodotus said the city of Babylon was square shaped, with each side being 14 miles long, while Ctesias, another ancient historian, said the distance around Babylon was a total of 42 miles.

The massive walls surrounding the city were wide enough to inspire an ancient poet to write, "I have gazed on the walls of impregnable Babylon, along which chariots may race."

We begin to be introduced to Babylon in the book of Genesis. After the worldwide flood of Noah's day, God instructed the people on the earth to spread out and inhabit the entire world. "Be fruitful, and multiply, and replenish the earth," God told Noah and his sons (Genesis 9:1).

A centralized population would make universal apostasy from God's truth much easier to effect, but with the devastating results of Satan's rebellion having only recently been witnessed, God's desire was to safeguard the human family. A decentralized population would be essential to the future spiritual well-being of the human family.

Led by Nimrod, the great-grandson of Noah, the inhabitants of the plain of Shinar rebelled against God and decided to remain clustered together rather than disperse as God had asked. "Let us build us a city and a tower, whose top may reach unto heaven; and let us make us a name, lest we be scattered abroad upon the face of the earth" (Genesis 11:4).

Their disobedience to God's express wishes exposed the world to heightened spiritual danger, prompting God to intervene to prevent a repeat of the decadence that prompted the devastating global flood.

God intentionally confused the speech of the people, so that instead of just one language being used on the plain of Shinar, a multiplicity of languages was suddenly being spoken. It isn't difficult to imagine how a massive building project would be utterly frustrated when it became all but impossible for fellow workers to communicate with each other.

"Therefore is the name of it called Babel, because the Lord did there confound the language of all the earth: and from thence did the Lord scatter them abroad upon the face of all the earth" (Genesis 11:9).

People were forced to associate by language group, leading to a dispersion of people to various points on the compass.

The word "Babel" means confusion, and it is from Babel that the word "Babylon" is derived. Confusion reigned at the Tower of Babel, and we will see that modern Babylon is mired in spiritual confusion. In fact, the Bible says that the doctrine of modern Babylon intoxicates people in the latter days of the world (Revelation 17:2).

The people at the Tower of Babel were characterized by self-exaltation. "Let us make us a name," the people said, an attitude very much like that of Satan himself before he was cast out of heaven (see Isaiah 14:13, 14).

In addition to self-exaltation, the people at the Tower of Babel were marked by self-righteousness. "Go to, let us build us a city and a tower, whose top may reach unto heaven..." (Genesis 11:4).

Their words sprang from rebellious hearts, unwilling to follow the leading of God. Like so many people since that time, these descendants of Noah certainly wanted to go to Heaven, but via methods of their own devising.

Ever since Cain brought his own offering to God just prior to the murder of Abel, multitudes have been worshiping God on their own terms rather than on the terms God has prescribed. That attitude reminds me of the man who insisted on buying his wife flowers to express his love to her, even though he knew she was allergic to flowers.

In today's world, vast numbers of people are seeking spiritual fulfillment independent of God's will, or even of God Himself, whereas the Bible makes it clear that the only way to spiritual maturity—the only way to Heaven—is through Jesus Christ.

No amount of human ingenuity can get a person an inch closer to the gates of Heaven. The builders of the Tower of Babel evidently didn't understand that, and it seems the point will also be lost on the Babylon of Earth's last days.

Later in the Old Testament, the kingdom of Babylon emerged, a heathen kingdom led by a ruthless king who oppressed the people of God. In fact, the book of Daniel records how in the year 605 BC, the armies of King Nebuchadnezzar attacked Jerusalem, laying the city waste, plundering its wealth, and capturing many of its citizens and transporting them to Babylon.

Captive Jews discovered that the city of Babylon was completely entrenched in paganism. Babylonians worshiped many different gods, including gods of water, the moon, the sky and the sun.

Many of today's religions feature aspects of pagan worship, including Christianity. The most common worship day among Christians, Sunday, is derived from the ancient Babylonian practice of the worship of the sun, and representations of the sun feature prominently in the architecture and worship services of many Christian churches today.

Integral to Babylon's religious worldview was the belief that the dead lived on after death, another idea that has gone on to substantially influence the modern world. Many religious groups in the Eastern, New Age and Christian traditions are founded upon the idea of an eternal soul surviving bodily death—a cornerstone belief of Babylonian religious thought.

The book of Daniel reveals that idolatry was a fundamental aspect of Babylonian religion and culture. Daniel chapter 3 records that King Nebuchadnezzar had his artisans construct a 90-foot-tall image of solid gold and commanded people to worship the image.

Speaking of the gods of Babylon, the prophet Isaiah wrote, "They lavish gold out of the bag, and weigh silver in the balance, and hire a goldsmith; and he maketh it a god: they fall down, yea, they worship" (Isaiah 46:6).

Idolatry is another Babylonian practice that we can see incorporated into many modern religions some thousands of years later.

Considering the characteristics of ancient Babylon and the people of the Tower of Babel is tremendously important as we study Babylon in Bible prophecy. In calling this end-time entity "Babylon", John was directing the minds of his readers back to the Babylon of the Old Testament.

Consideration of the Babylon of old will help us understand the Babylon ahead. And what makes this even more important is knowing that the Babylon of the book of Revelation and the antichrist beast of Bible prophecy are one and the same.

As we review some of the characteristics of ancient Babylon, here's what we see:

Ancient Babylon

- Was in rebellion against God's Word.
- Relied on righteousness by works.
- Indulged in self-exaltation.
- Is characterized by confusion.
- Was immersed in paganism.
- Engaged in sun worship.
- Believed in the immortality of the soul.
- Practiced idolatry.

It can be expected that modern Babylon will possess many of the same characteristics of ancient Babylon. That certain facets of the religion of old Babylon have bled over into many of today's religious faiths should not come as a surprise. After all, Babylon is rising.

Chapter Three

WHERE THERE'S SMOKE...

I remember as a child deciding I was going to read the book of Revelation and figure out what it meant. Looking back, I'm not sure where my motivation came from (other than the prompting of the Holy Spirit), but I distinctly recall taking out the big family Bible and opening it to its final book.

This big family Bible—gold-edged pages, gorgeously illustrated, beautifully laid out—didn't get a lot of use, and I thought it would be a good idea for me to not only use it, but get to the bottom of what some of it meant.

It didn't take me long to realize that I wasn't going to figure out Revelation any time soon. Beasts and kings, locusts and scorpions, seals and trumpets, plagues...I wondered how anyone could *ever* figure it out. But believing that the Bible really is the Word of God, I knew it had to mean something. Maybe someday I'd be able to understand.

As I got older I was intrigued as I encountered various authors who were confident they had deciphered Revelation's true meaning. But while I was certainly no Bible expert, it often seemed to me that the concrete opinions of many so-called "experts" were nothing more than speculation.

It was about this time that talk started swirling about the "beast" of Bible prophecy. Someone or something was going to cause a lot of trouble for God's people in the end times. Someone or something was going to bring some massive deceptions into the word, the mark of the beast being one of them.

I didn't have a clue who or what that beast was going to be, and then word started spreading that a supercomputer in Belgium was so powerful and so far-reaching and so technologically advanced that it was somehow going to be the great villain at the end of time.

A computer? The beast? The *antichrist*? As little as I knew, it seemed unlikely that a computer was going to be one of the primary troublemakers of human history. (Little did I know that years later I would own a computer or two that would often act as though it were an agent of the devil...)

How a computer was going to be the last-days beast of Bible prophecy was beyond me, but back in those days, computers were enigmatic enough in the eyes of many people for this theory to actually take hold. And it turned out that this would be just one of many interesting interpretations I would hear on the subject.

When looking to understand some of the mysteries of Bible prophecy, a simple rule of thumb is to simply *read* the book of Revelation, and see for yourself what it says. You'll read in Revelation chapter 13 about the mark of the *beast*. The chapter says nothing at all about the mark of the *computer*.

To understand the idea of the *beast* of Bible prophecy, we remember that the prophet Daniel clearly defined a beast as a symbol used in prophecy to represent a king, or more explicitly, a *kingdom*. You'll read that in Daniel 7:17 and Daniel 7:23. It is very plainly stated.

Which raises in my mind a puzzling and a somewhat troubling question: if it is so clear in the Bible that a beast is a prophetic symbol that represents a kingdom or a nation, how is it that so many Bible teachers have got this so wrong?

Some years ago I saw a well-known prophecy teacher on a television program state emphatically that "whenever you see that word 'beast' written in the book of Revelation, it is referring to a man." In spite of the Bible evidence—"the fourth beast shall be the fourth kingdom upon earth" (Daniel 7:23)—there's no question that many people believed what he said.

The book of Revelation draws heavily from the Old Testament, with almost three-quarters of its verses containing quotes from—or references to—the Old Testament. The apocalyptic imagery in Revelation draws solidly from the Old Testament, especially from the book of Daniel.

When John wrote Revelation, he wrote much of it in a kind of code, using symbols and images to represent the meaning of what he was saying. This code was designed to take people back to the Old Testament Scriptures, where they would find a fuller meaning of what he was writing about.

For instance, when he was writing the opening verses of Revelation 13, he wrote that a beast would rise up out of the sea, and that it would be like a leopard, that its feet would resemble the feet of a bear, and that it would have a mouth much like that of a lion (Revelation 13:2).

Anyone reading this back in John's day would immediately say, "Oh, we see what he is talking about. He is saying a nation is going to rise up in a populated part of the world, and it would resemble in some way the kingdoms of Greece, Medo-Persia and Babylon."

They would know that a beast represents a nation; that the sea in prophecy represents multitudes of people (see Revelation 17:15); that the leopard image came straight from Daniel where it represented the kingdom of Greece (Daniel 7:6); that the bear image alluded to the kingdom of Medo-Persia (Daniel 7:5); and that the lion represented the kingdom of Babylon (Daniel 7:4).

It was as though John was utilizing a form of shorthand. By saying "Babylon" in the Old Testament, he could succinctly transmit to his readers the idea he was trying to convey. They would read "Babylon" and say to themselves, "Okay, I understand the type of kingdom he is talking about. It is going to be much like the kingdom of Babylon in the Old Testament, which long ago did thus and so..."

Rather than guessing that a beast represents a man, or a gigantic computer, it is important to interpret the Bible according to sound rules of Biblical interpretation, not guesswork and conjecture.

But that hasn't stopped the speculators.

Years ago some thought Adolph Hitler was the antichrist. While it isn't hard to see why people might have thought that, history shows that as ghastly as his crimes were, Hitler certainly wasn't the prophesied antichrist of the Bible.

Another theory that gained some traction was the idea that former US Secretary of State Henry Kissinger was the Biblical antichrist. Just how Mr. Kissinger was supposed to have fulfilled the criteria for being the antichrist is beyond me, but his being a Jewish emigrant from Germany was enough to incite some people to believe that he was "the one". Again, history has demonstrated that Henry Kissinger is certainly not a prophetic figure at all. The whole notion was completely ludicrous.

But what we see is that intelligent people with free access to the Bible are capable of arriving at completely unrealistic positions that have no basis in fact whatsoever. Many respected people genuinely believed Henry Kissinger was a major prophetic player, even though there was never, ever any basis in fact for the idea.

Former President Ronald Reagan was said to be the antichrist. The reason? Because his name—Ronald Wilson Reagan—is made up of three words with six letters in each word: six, six, six.

It Is Written's ministry headquarters is located only a couple of miles from where former President Reagan is now buried, which itself suggests that former President Reagan never was the antichrist of Bible prophecy. That is, he has been dead since 2004. Surely there were times when his political opponents thought his ideas were out of this world, but President Reagan? The *antichrist*? The speculators were wrong again.

A number of years ago, I was discussing this subject in a Bible prophecy lecture series when I was approached by an excited man who was anxious to help me understand what he thought were the errors in my thinking.

"You don't understand John! The beast of Bible prophecy is...Procter & Gamble!"

He was referring to the enormous multinational corporation that makes laundry detergent, paper towels, cosmetics and diapers, among other things. I remember thinking, "You mean if I eat any more Pringles [a P&G product], I'll end up with the mark of the beast?" I asked him to flesh out his theory a little.

"John" he said, "do you know where Procter & Gamble is headquartered?"

"Oh no," I said, "you can't be serious..."

He was. "Cincinnati!" he hooted triumphantly. "Cincinnati! And the Bible says the antichrist is the man of *sin*!"

"The man of sin, not the man of *Cincinnati*!" I said to him.

My attempts at reason were of no avail. He went on his way determinedly suspicious of the corporate giant.

Evidently, someone once looked at Procter & Gamble's corporate logo—at one time a bearded "man in the moon" looking off toward 13 stars—and deduced that the company had something to do with the dark side. Time and lawsuits have both demonstrated that the Procter & Gamble company is not featured in the Bible's last book.

While it isn't difficult to demonstrate that politicians and corporations aren't implicated in the book of Revelation—a beast is a nation, remember—it is a different matter when it comes to secret societies such as the Freemasons and the Illuminati.

Perhaps one reason for this is their very nature. They're *secretive*. And anyone living in the shadows can rightly or wrongly expect to be the target of conjecture and speculation.

There are approximately 2 million Freemasons in the United States who, some say, go so far as to knowingly worship the devil himself. While it isn't always easy to know the private worship practices of individuals, it is said by some that many of the rituals of Freemasonry are anchored in paganism and include practices that are mired in the occult.

Freemasons describe themselves as being part of a fraternity that is "dedicated to the Brotherhood of Man under the Fatherhood of a Supreme Being". Although Masons deny Freemasonry is a religion, there seems to be plenty in the "brotherhood" of a religious nature.

Many powerful men have been Freemasons, including presidents of the United States—such as George

Washington, Franklin D. Roosevelt, Theodore Roosevelt, Harry S. Truman and Andrew Jackson—and leaders in business and industry.

This would suggest at the very least that Freemasons have had a considerable impact on the United States and its policies. But does this mean Freemasonry is a major figure when it comes to the fulfillment of Bible prophecy? The difficulty with determining the truth about organizations like the Freemasons is that much of what Masons do is shrouded in concealment.

But we must keep in mind that in terms of the book of Revelation, the key figures in last-days prophecy are the beast—which must, by definition, be a nation—the dragon and the false prophet, none of which can possibly be the organization of Freemasonry.

It is true that much of what is known of Freemasonry is deeply troubling to many Christians, but while Masons have clearly had a considerable influence in business and politics, Freemasonry itself is not directly implicated in end-time Bible prophecy.

The same is true of organizations and groups such as the Bilderberg Group, the Council on Foreign Relations and the Illuminati. If you've never heard of these groups, rest assured that there are numerous individuals who are convinced they are the bogeymen of Earth's final days.

While some researchers claim to have unearthed information implicating these bodies as co-conspirators in an end-time New World Order, concrete information on these groups and their activities is not easy to find. And again, we point out that the book of Revelation does not directly implicate them in any end-time prophetic scenario.

I'm not suggesting that any of the shadowy, secretive organizations in the world are above reproach, but I believe there's a need to be responsible when interpreting Bible prophecy.

The temptation to implicate mysterious groups in end-time global collusion is real, as certain organizations are secretive and—apparently—influential. In some cases it seems they have access to leaders at the highest echelons of influence and power. They just *have* to be part of Earth's last great deception, right?

There's no question that the devil is cunning and clever. When the attention of the world ought to be on what really matters in Earth's last days, large numbers of people are spending their time focusing on shadowy groups about whom rather little is known. This is especially true when it comes to their apparently nefarious plans to bring about chaos and spiritual confusion at the end of time.

Is it possible that there are organizations on the planet that give the devil an assist as he works through the real spiritual villains of Earth's final hours? That's certainly possible. But in trying to associate these groups with the major prophecies in the book of Revelation, large numbers of people are essentially wasting their energy by barking up the wrong spiritual tree.

It is important that we understand where the battle is and where the battle is not in Earth's final hours. Paul made very clear that we wrestle "not with flesh and blood" but "against spiritual wickedness in high places" (Ephesians 6:12), meaning that the largest spiritual battles we face are not with human beings but with the dark forces of the demon world.

While it is true that Satan certainly works through organizations to further his aims, the key issues brought to light in the final hours of Earth's history do not focus on businessmen seeking great wealth or statesmen seeking political advantage.

What we have in the book of Revelation is the culmination of Satan's attempt to receive the worship of the world. The prophet Isaiah records that long ago, Satan said in his heart:

"I will ascend into heaven, I will exalt my throne above the stars of God: I will sit also upon the mount of the congregation, in the sides of the north: I will ascend above the heights of the clouds; I will be like the Most High" (Isaiah 14:13, 14).

For some inexplicable reason, a created being, Lucifer, came to the place where he wanted to receive the worship due only to God. He wanted to hold the preeminent place in the universe, and his madness and hate and jealousy and self-centeredness led him to the place where he was ultimately evicted from Heaven.

Unsuccessful in receiving the worship he desired, Satan has come to Earth determined to receive the worship he was unable to secure in Heaven. Accompanied by the angels who rebelled with him against the government of God, Satan now not only attacks the objects of God's love, but also seeks to fix upon them a mark of their loyalty to him—the mark of the beast.

Planet Earth is involved in a spiritual crisis, where a jealous devil is trying desperately to take total control of planet Earth, prevent people from being saved eternally, and demonstrate that God is unfair and unjust—charges he made in Heaven and repeated in the Garden of Eden.

His masterpiece of deception is still to be unleashed upon an unsuspecting world. Ultimately, he will work through Babylon—the beast, the antichrist, the man of sin—to bring his greatest deceptions to the world and cause as many as he can to be eternally separated from God.

Unquestionably, there are many groups, organizations or individuals on Earth today with impure motives and illegitimate modes of operation. But what Satan has been doing in recent years—as interest in Bible prophecy has been increasing—is causing people to look in all the wrong places for all the wrong things.

Christians who could know better are busy worrying about computers, politicians and business elites bringing spiritual crisis to the world, while Satan flies under the radar and his greatest deceptions—now starting to come to maturity—are ignored and largely unrecognized.

In 1993, professional basketball's Chicago Bulls were vying to win their third straight National Basketball Association championship title. With Michael Jordan on their team—the greatest player in the history of the game—Chicago was about as sure a bet as a team could be in a major sporting event.

Holding a three-games-to-two lead over Phoenix and needing just one more win to retain their championship title (and become only the third team in history to win the NBA title three years in a row), it seemed obvious what Chicago would—and should—do.

Michael Jordan had been red hot during this finals series, averaging about 43 points per game: with only seconds to go in the game, everybody watching just *knew* the ball was going to Michael Jordan to attempt a game-winning shot.

Chicago was trailing by two points: a basket now would make the score 98-98, while a three-point shot would put the Bulls ahead by one and win the game and the series.

Led by Charles Barkley, another of the game's greats, the Phoenix Suns—knowing they had to eliminate Chicago's lethal scoring threat—assigned two defenders to Jordan in an effort to keep him from scoring.

They also knew that if Jordan couldn't get a clear shot at the basket, he would likely look to get the ball to Scottie Pippen, so Phoenix defended Pippen aggressively as well. The two best players on the Chicago team—their two biggest scoring threats—were covered. Phoenix felt it was in a good position.

Unable to shoot, Michael Jordan passed the ball to Pippen, who in turn unloaded the ball to Chicago's next highest scorer, Horace Grant. But Grant was also covered by Phoenix's stifling defense.

Phoenix had identified Chicago's danger men and was preventing them from getting off a game-winning shot. Surely this game—now with less than five seconds left—would be won by Phoenix, and there would be a deciding game seven a day or two later back in Chicago.

Except for one thing. Phoenix, while guarding some key danger men, had ignored one player. John Paxson, then 32 years old and averaging just seven points a game, took the ball behind the three-point line on a pass from Grant and launched the ball toward the basket.

As the final seconds ticked away, the Phoenix Suns players could only stand and watch their chance at victory slip from their grasp. They had been aggressively defending the Bulls' standout players, while leaving the real danger man unmarked. John Paxson's shot won the game—and the NBA finals—for Chicago. While Phoenix was anticipating trouble from one area of the court, they did not realize that the greatest danger at the time was lurking elsewhere, unrecognized.

Many Christians are doing the same thing today. While the Bible talks about a beast with a mark, a beast that will deceive the world and whose followers will be lost when Jesus returns, many people are looking for trouble in all the wrong places.

Which is not to say that the focus of their attention is harmless. There was a good chance Jordan or Pippen would make the game-winning basket for Chicago. It made sense for the Phoenix team to guard them. But while people are fretting about shadowy, secretive groups with barely understood modes of operation, they're missing the point as to where the end-time danger really is.

No, Ronald Reagan was never going to be the beast of Bible prophecy. Neither was Mikhail Gorbachev or Saddam Hussein or King Juan Carlos of Spain.

(Yes, people really believed that.) And whatever their agenda and whatever their failings may be, the Masons and the Illuminati and other secretive organizations are not the major players in the Bible's final book.

It is said that where there's smoke, there's fire. But sometimes, where there's smoke, there's only smoke.

It is important for Bible students to take the time to carefully consider what God's Word says. Because Babylon is rising.

Chapter Four

CONSPIRACY

I remember it like it was yesterday. I got up in the morning, spent my devotional time with God, and then went to check my e-mail. Still chained to dialup Internet access, I was used to slow connections, but this morning it was even slower than usual. My connection came through so slowly I thought there was a problem with my computer.

When headlines finally started appearing on my screen, I couldn't believe what I was reading. "Plane Crashes Into World Trade Center." I called out to Melissa, "Oh no, there's been a disastrous accident!"

She could tell by the tone of my voice that this was something serious. We both gazed at the computer screen in utter disbelief, and our shock only deepened as the minutes passed. "A terrorist attack...they say there could be thousands dead..."

Because we didn't have a television at the little home in which we were staying at the time, we headed to the local Walmart and gathered with several others around a TV in the electronics department. There, a group of strangers bonded together during a tragedy we all sensed was going to inexorably change our lives.

It didn't take long for the conspiracy theorists to start talking. The hideous, murderous plot was not the brainchild of Muslim extremists, they said, but of the United States government! They claimed it was a conspiracy and that the plane crashes couldn't possibly have caused the damage that was done.

While the tragedy raised any number of puzzling questions, various scientific organizations have affirmed that the devastation caused at the World Trade Center in New York City was the result of jet fuel-laden aircraft colliding with the skyscrapers.

In spite of that, some people remain dissatisfied with the official version of events, still convinced that there is more to the collapse of the Twin Towers and the carnage at the Pentagon than what we've been told. Many people are certain that 9/11 was the result of a massive *conspiracy*.

Conspiracy theorists also claim Neil Armstrong never walked on the moon, and that the moon landings were a hoax. Conspiracists also claim that global elites purposely introduced the AIDS virus, that Princess Diana's death was not the result of an accident and that the United States government knew ahead of time that Pearl Harbor was going to be bombed.

I'm convinced the destruction of the Twin Towers in 2001 *was* part of a massive conspiracy. It was a carefully planned, expertly executed conspiracy, the truth of which the general public has been told very little about.

In this chapter, we'll lift the lid on the greatest conspiracy ever. And if we discover who was really behind the tragedy of 9/11, we'll understand some important things about the last great crisis confronting humanity.

The majority of people don't even want to believe such things as conspiracy theories, but the claims and the questions conspiracy theorists raise do make a point: sometimes there are things going on behind the scenes that we in front of the scenes don't witness. Very often, what you see doesn't adequately represent what is actually taking place.

Jews in Germany could see the increase in Nazi troops and knew their liberties were being seriously curtailed. But they didn't know that what they were seeing would add up to what they could not see—behind high fences in concentration camps.

The German war machine deliberately misled the entire world into thinking that their actions were not nearly as hideous as they were in actuality. Hitler's Nazis conspired to mislead the world while they marched determinedly toward world dominion.

Should what we see taking place in the world today be accepted at face value, or is there a "story behind the story", more to the headlines than meets the eye? The fact is that the master conspirator—the brains behind the chaos being experienced in the world today, the master manipulator engineering the crisis of all crises—is Satan himself.

Let's keep in mind a couple of incontrovertible facts. Speaking of a time shortly before the return of Jesus, the Bible says Satan will employ agencies to "go forth unto the kings of the earth and of the whole world, to gather them to the battle of that great day of God Almighty" (Revelation 16:14).

A *gathering* will take place before Jesus returns. Such a gathering can't come from out of nowhere and happen in an instant. Rather, this gathering will be the culmination of a prolonged strategy during which Satan grooms the world—setting the world up to be swept away in history's final great delusion.

The book of Revelation says that "all the world" will "wonder after" [marvel at] the beast (Revelation 13:3). Revelation 13:8 says that "all that dwell upon the earth shall worship him", and Revelation 18 explicitly states that governments of the world will be united in an illicit relationship with Babylon.

That can't possibly just happen overnight. There has to be a period of time during which developments will take place that set the world up for that time.

For example, Apple didn't become the world's biggest technology company overnight. Born in 1976 near San Jose, Calif., Apple originally sold "computers" that were little more than a motherboard—with no screen and no keyboard.

Today, that would hardly seem like the surefire path to global domination, but over time—with the development of new products like the Macintosh computer—Apple began to win over legions of computer users.

However, in the early 1990s, Apple was all but irrelevant to anyone but a die-hard Apple fanatic. As strange as it now seems, Apple's future was, at one time, in serious jeopardy.

But Apple developed long-term plans for future success. It brought company co-founder Steve Jobs back into the Apple fold, and began to acquire companies and roll out new products. The iMac and the phenomenally successful iPod were followed by the iPhone and the iPad. Still based in Cupertino but now with 50,000 employees worldwide and with annual revenues of around $65 billion, Apple rules the technology world.

How did the Apple of the 1970s become the Apple of the 21st century? It happened slowly but surely, and with a few missteps along the way. But ever since Apple's inception, the company has been committed to producing excellent, must-have products. Over time, their strategy has led them to the top of the technological mountain, and Apple is now the most valuable technology company in the world.

If you'll pardon the analogy (and PC users no doubt will), Satan's march toward global domination can be expected to be a series of calculated moves, innovations, developments, and reactions to societal trends and forces.

You can expect that just like a multinational technology company, or like a political party strategizing an ascension to power, Satan will work behind the scenes to prepare this world to accept his leadership and receive the mark of his authority.

The truth is, he has been working toward this for thousands of years. He's been slowly, almost imperceptibly, leading the people of planet Earth to the place where they'll be led away from allegiance to God and will instead choose loyalty to history's first rebel.

Consider with me how Satan has been grooming the planet in preparation for his grab at power.

The book of Revelation states that before the return of Jesus, those who refuse to worship the beast will be prevented from buying and selling. I've had a number of people ask me over the years, "And just how is he going to manage that?"

There's no question that back in the days of mechanical cash registers, this seemed outside the realms of possibility. Go back a couple of hundred years and the idea seemed entirely preposterous.

But now? In today's electronic economy, you can do your banking online or over the phone, and you can buy anything you need on the Internet, without exchanging a single dollar bill.

Cash isn't used like it used to be—most people conduct transactions using credit cards, debit cards or checks. Few people are paid by their employer in cash. One's wages are almost always direct-deposited into a bank account, and cash is usually accessed via ATM.

This being so, how difficult would it be for someone in authority to prevent people from buying and selling? With the click of a mouse, any authorized bank employee could effectively prevent you from buying and selling. Once you burned through your cash and emptied your piggy bank, you'd be back to bartering like people did hundreds of years ago.

Society has gone increasingly cashless over the last two or three decades, and rumors have circulated for years that we'll go even further in that direction. We've been told by some that cash will disappear in favor of rechargeable cards. It has been said by others that people will have a silicon chip implanted under their skin that will be used to conduct business transactions.

While there's really no way of knowing how likely either scenario is, modern technology has catapulted them into the realms of possibility. What's the net result of this march toward progress?

On one hand, we're better off because financial transactions become easier and more convenient, and in some ways we are protected from theft and loss to a greater extent than our grandparents were. But the very things that mean progress also leave us incredibly vulnerable to those who will one day seek to control how you buy and sell. If everything is electronically managed, it just takes a tiny amount of electronic intervention, and your financial assets are frozen.

This is not a new idea. In recent history, various nations have imposed economic embargoes against regimes in South Africa, Cuba and other countries. The purpose of economic sanctions is to change behavior—to convince certain people to alter their course of action.

This is the purpose of the economic sanctions levied in Revelation chapter 13. One hundred years ago, wholesale economic sanctions would have been very difficult to effect.

But in today's electronic age, it would not be hard at all.

I remember a young lady attending a seminar I held in Iowa years ago excitedly explaining to me how the last-days crisis was going to play out.

"There's a company," she told me sincerely, "that has developed a tiny silicon chip that can actually be injected under the skin of a human being. That chip can contain every bit of information about you that there is, and it's only with that chip under your skin that a person is going to be able to buy and sell."

And then came the kicker: "And you know what this is called?"

I didn't need to be told. I knew exactly where she was going.

"It's going to be called...the Beast! See?"

I have to admit I did see, only too clearly. What I could see was what happens when people seize half-truths and marry them to whole errors. The last great deception to face the Earth revolves around whether or not you're unfortunate enough to get an injection in your hand? I don't think so.

One thing we can know for sure: whatever happens to the economies of the world, and whatever innovations are introduced in the area of buying and selling, these things are not the mark of the beast.

Contrary to the insistence of some of the speculators that move among us, a "cashless society" or a "smart card" is *not* the mark of the beast. Remember, a prohibition against buying and selling is not the mark of the beast, but a means of coercing people to *receive* the mark of the beast. The two ideas are related, but decidedly different.

That having been said, it is easy to see how good technology could easily be used for nefarious purposes. Without a doubt, that's what will happen before the Lord returns.

I welcome technological advancements that make it easier for me to manage my finances and protect me from fraud and theft. But Satan, the great conspirator, has planned for millennia to tighten the screws on God's people in Earth's last days.

He has planned for eons to make it impossible for people to buy and sell unless they are loyal to him and disloyal to God. And over time, he has encouraged the development of technology so that masses of people could be effectively prevented from buying and selling.

So, as my children used to say when they were younger, "Are we there yet?"

The truth is that the future has arrived. We're already there. We don't have to wait for any new technologies to be developed before this end-time scenario can be enacted.

You've likely experienced this already in your own life: you put the card into the slot at a gas station and a message pops up telling you there's a problem with your card, and you can't buy gas. Or you go to the hole-in-the-wall machine and insert your card, and the machine tells you that for some reason it can't give you any money. And there goes your night on the town. Or you go to pay for your groceries and the cashier informs you they don't accept out-of-town checks, leaving you standing in line with a cart full of groceries and a knot in your stomach.

Are the banks running the world into the ground? Are the Rockefellers and the Rothschilds plotting to preside over the economies of the world? To be honest, I have no idea. And whether they are or are not is of zero spiritual consequence.

Men may plan and scheme and plot, but the great conspirator is Satan himself. As technology advances, as the banking systems consolidate, as wealth is centralized, Satan waits to pounce like a cat stalking a mouse.

When the time is right, and Earth's last great deception is ready to be rolled out, everything will be in place to enable Satan to manipulate the world's economy, and to control buying and selling.

There are other aspects of the present-day economic situation that are covered in the fingerprints of the master conspirator. Americans with credit cards owe about $1 trillion dollars in credit card debt. The average credit card holder in this country owes thousands of dollars to credit card companies—in many cases, tens of thousands.

People who are in debt are not people who are ultimately in control of their lives. The Bible says that the "borrower is servant to the lender" (Proverbs 22:7). A runaway housing market was a lot of fun for a lot of people for a few years, but it ended up being a millstone around the necks of tens of thousands of homeowners who woke up one morning to discover their homes were no longer worth what was owed on them.

Is Satan working in this? You can be sure he is. Not only because he wants to ruin lives, rob people of happiness and load people up with guilt—but also because he fully intends to deprive people of the control they have over their financial destiny.

It is no coincidence that this close to the return of Jesus, more people than ever before are drowning in debt. For decades Satan has fostered an attitude of "have all you want, and have it now."

Greed is rampant in society today, and greed leads to debt, and debt can lead to ruin, and ruin in a time of crisis leaves a person entirely vulnerable. What happens in the last days when people are unable to pay their debts, and are—essentially—the property of a banking system to which they owe impossible amounts of money?

They'll be slaves to the system, totally without freedom to make choices for themselves regarding the direction of their lives. Just how Satan planned. Not a good place to be during the time of Earth's last crisis.

And have you noticed how closely interrelated the economies of the nations of the world are? When the American stock market tumbled in 1989, other countries of the world fell into a funk.

In recent years we've seen how economic crises in relatively small nations have had a big impact on the economic strength of other, much larger nations. The recent credit crunch has been referred to as a *global* credit crunch. Someone is working behind the scenes to manipulate economies for his own end. And that "someone" is Satan.

And consider the way society is now structured. When God created the world, Adam and Eve lived in a garden. They were rural folk. No city in the world amassed a population of 200,000 people until Babylon did so in about 612 BC. Some say 8th century Baghdad was the first city to reach a population of 1 million, and that number was probably not surpassed until the 19th century by London.

Today, more than half of the world's population lives in cities. While it is difficult to find consistency among population figures, many sources list the population of the Tokyo metro area at about 34 million. The metropolitan areas of Seoul, Mexico City and New York City are all at or above 20 million, with around 25 metro areas having a population of 10 million or more.

It doesn't take a rocket scientist to figure out that people jammed into the world's teeming megalopolises are incredibly vulnerable to shortages and supply problems (not to mention social problems). If you have land, you can grow your own food. But what if you're living on the ninth floor of an apartment building?

In addition to providing a reliable food source, the agrarian lifestyle of yesteryear provided mass employment. In ancient times, unemployment was rare and nobody received welfare payments from the government.

Today, unemployment numbers are sky high. In the United States, millions of people receive government assistance, and the government is the nation's largest employer. Please don't think I'm criticizing any of that. My point is that the amount of people out of work or relying on the government for an income makes people very vulnerable to changes in the economy or to government policies—just as Satan would like people to be.

If you were the devil and you were looking to control people financially, wouldn't you want to orchestrate a situation where masses of people lived where they were especially vulnerable and were reliant on others for survival? Yes, you would. And that's where we are today. The master conspirator has done a very effective job of setting people up for Earth's last great crisis.

In our increasingly Orwellian world, Big Brother is definitely watching you. Anyone living in a city of any size at all is frequently observed by surveillance cameras in lobbies and businesses and motels and on streets all over town.

Security cameras have of course been used to great effect to bring criminals to justice, which most anyone would applaud. But with surveillance cameras now being used even in residential areas, it isn't hard to see that the potential exists for such technology to be misused.

Recently, the *New York Times* reported that a German Green party politician named Malte Spitz discovered that his cell phone company, Deutsche Telekom, had recorded and saved his longitude and latitude coordinates more than 35,000 times. While most people realize cell phone companies need to keep track of us to provide optimum service, many people—like Mr. Spitz—are surprised to know they are being tracked via their cell phone.

Could there be a master conspirator at work in this? Or does it not matter? It might not, except that in Earth's final days, the good guys are widely perceived as the bad guys. The devil will succeed in convincing the masses that the minority—a group of God's faithful people—are in fact the cause of trouble and not blessing.

It isn't difficult to imagine good technology being used for bad purposes. And what is interesting is that people all over the world have shown themselves to be remarkably accepting of intrusions into their personal privacy.

In the interests of national security, it is now common at airports around the United States for full-body image detectors to capture nude images of travelers. To be sure, these images don't rival Olan Mills for clarity. They're virtual photographs. But can you imagine the reaction a generation ago if a security guard at an airport had insisted on capturing naked images of travelers? With the alternative being an invasive, full-body pat down?

How did we get to this place? Think September 11, 2001—the day that changed the world. Preventing similar terrors is necessarily an extremely high priority for governments around the world, and Satan, the master conspirator, knew ahead of time that this would be the case.

While there are obviously very good reasons for this eroding of individual privacy, Satan correctly calculated that a worldwide terror alert would lead people to trade liberty for safety—making it far easier for him to enforce his plans for Earth's final days.

And because the last great crisis to come upon the world will be religious in nature, and focused on worship, it is no surprise that Satan has thrust offbeat religious minorities into the world's spotlight.

The Waco tragedy in 1993 demonstrated that groups perceived as religious extremists garner very little public sympathy. In today's climate of fear and mistrust, there's a low tolerance for religious groups that are out of the mainstream. But what if a religious minority were actually in the right and not in the wrong? Based on what we read in the book of Revelation, it won't be long until we find out.

And really, that's all okay. It's okay because God's people have never had to rely on their own inventiveness, their own wits, and their own schemes and plans in order to be safe. As the Bible says, "God is our refuge and strength" (Psalm 46:1).

Technology, security, governments and banks are not the enemies of God's people. Paul was very clear when he wrote to the Ephesians that "we wrestle not against flesh and blood, but against principalities, against powers, against the rulers of the darkness of this world" (Ephesians 6:12).

The master conspirator, Satan, is slowly but surely manipulating world events so he can bring the world to the place where "all the world wondered after the beast" (Revelation 13:3).

Ultimately, anyone at all—the super-rich, American presidents, leaders in society, bankers, doctors, lawyers, school teachers and bus drivers—anyone who is not surrendered to God will be a pawn in Satan's game, to aid the rise of Babylon and rally against the people of God.

Jesus Himself said, "He that is not with me is against me, and he that gathereth not with me scattereth abroad" (Matthew 12:30).

Later in Matthew's gospel, Jesus talks about the people on Earth in the last days, referring to them as wheat and tares, good fish and bad fish, sheep and goats. In Revelation, John identifies the same two groups, this time referring to them as those who receive the mark of the beast, and those who receive the seal of God.

About 20 years ago, while living in London, I met up with an old high-school friend in Covent Garden, where a variety of street performers were entertaining the crowds of people. An illusionist caught our eye, and we stopped to watch him for a while.

What we saw absolutely amazed us both. Standing his assistant on a low step, he placed a broom under each of her arms and caused her to "fall asleep". He then removed the step, and one of the brooms—leaving her supported by a single broom under her left arm with both feet off the ground. He then lifted her feet at a right angle to the broom, leaving her suspended in midair perpendicular to the broom.

We were totally astounded. As far as we could tell, the illusionist had caused a young woman to float in the air supported by only a thin piece of wood positioned at one end of her body. What we saw defied gravity, physics and logic. The entire crowd was transfixed.

To this day, I know that I saw what I saw. But I don't know how the illusion was done. There was something going on behind the scenes that I did not see—that I could not see—that made it possible for the performer to wow the audience gathered there that sunny English afternoon.

We don't always know what is going on behind the scenes, but we can be certain that at this moment the great conspirator is working tirelessly to draw the inhabitants of planet Earth into his net of deception. There is no question: Babylon is rising.

Chapter Five

WHO IS BABYLON?

Without question, one of the most reviled men in all of history is Adolph Hitler. As the Chancellor of Germany from 1933 to 1945, Hitler headed the National Socialist German Workers' Party, better known as the Nazis.

In his pursuit of global domination, he presided over the extermination of an estimated 6 million Jews, approximately 1 million Romani, and many thousands of others Hitler felt ran counter to his ideology.

As hideous as Hitler's murderous exploits were, they were eclipsed in number by Joseph Stalin, the former leader of the Soviet Union. Depending on which historian you read, Stalin is said to have been responsible for the deaths of between 15-30 million people.

The phenomenon of the cruel tyrant is by no means a new one. Although he died at the relatively young age of 30, the Roman Emperor Nero distinguished himself and his reign as Emperor by malevolence and brutality.

He executed not only his own mother and stepbrother, but in all likelihood started the fire that destroyed much of the city of ancient Rome.

The torching of Rome left Nero highly unpopular with his subjects, and realizing he needed a scapegoat, Nero suggested that the Christians in Rome were responsible for its destruction. As a result, Christians were rounded up and murdered in astonishingly inhumane ways.

The Roman persecution of the early church was so intense that the Christians began to use code words to describe the city. In the Bible, Peter finishes his first letter to his readers with a cryptic greeting from a mysterious Christian church:

"She who is in Babylon, elect together with you, greets you; and so does Mark my son" (1 Peter 5:13).

Who could Peter be talking about when he mentions a group of people in *Babylon*? These believers cannot have been a church group in the literal city of Babylon, because the city of Babylon had been in ruins since the days of Alexander the Great.

If you check the scholarly footnotes of many editions of the Bible, you'll find that a large amount of Bible scholars believe "Babylon" is code for the city of Rome.

When John wrote the book of Revelation some years after Peter wrote his letters, Roman persecution against the church was still burning hot. After a botched execution attempt, John was exiled to the Island of Patmos, and it was there that the material for Revelation was born.

John used the name of a historical persecuting power to symbolize the great persecuting power of the last days of Earth's history.

In the 17th chapter of Revelation, he makes reference to a woman with a mysterious inscription on her forehead:

"And on her forehead a name was written: Mystery, Babylon the Great, the mother of harlots and abominations of the earth. And I saw the woman drunken with the blood of the saints, and with the blood of the martyrs of Jesus: and when I saw her, I wondered with great admiration" (Revelation 17:5, 6).

An angel explains to John what the imagery means.

"And here is the mind which hath wisdom. The seven heads are seven mountains on which the woman sitteth" (Revelation 17:9).

And again, in verse 18:

"And the woman which thou sawest is that great city, which reigneth over the kings of the earth" (Revelation 17:18).

The woman, according to the Bible itself, is a city that sits on seven hills and reigns over the kings of the Earth. In all of human history, there is only one city that matches that description, and that is Rome, the city of seven hills.

Writing some time in the second century AD, the Christian apologist Tertullian confirms what the early Christians understood by the code word "Babylon".

"So, again, Babylon, in our own John, is a figure of the city Rome, as being equally great and proud of her sway, and triumphant over the saints" (Tertullian, Answers to the Jews, Chapter 9).

It is significant that ancient Rome is represented as "Babylon". And it is equally significant that Babylon is referred to as a woman. In Bible prophecy, a *woman* is frequently used to represent a church.

Writing to the church at Corinth, Paul said, "For I am jealous over you with godly jealousy: for I have espoused you to one husband, that I may present you as a chaste virgin to Christ" (2 Corinthians 11:2).

In Jeremiah 6:2 we read, "I have likened the daughter of Zion to a comely and delicate woman."

It is fascinating that the book of Revelation presents two women—one, a pure woman representing God's church (see Revelation 12:1, 2, 17). The other is an immoral woman who has multiple immoral daughters (Revelation 17:1, 5).

This second woman is guilty of committing spiritual adultery—"cheating" on God, as it were.

So if "Babylon" is a code word for the Roman Empire, then in what sense could Rome be guilty of spiritual adultery? It is clear that when John is writing about Babylon, he's not just talking about the old, pagan Roman Empire.

There's a fascinating prediction found in Paul's second letter to the Thessalonians, in chapter 2.

"Let no one deceive you by any means; for that Day will not come unless the falling away comes first, and the man of sin is revealed, the son of perdition, who opposes and exalts himself above all that is called God or that is worshiped, so that he sits as God in the temple of God, showing himself that he is God (2 Thessalonians 2:3, 4).

Paul states that "the man of sin"—the same power as the "beast" in Revelation 13 and Babylon in Revelation 17—would make his entrance onto the world scene before the Second Coming of Christ, and he then provides more details on the timing of that event. Notice what he says:

"Do you not remember that when I was still with you I told you these things? And now you know what is restraining, that he may be revealed in his own time. For the mystery of lawlessness is already at work; only He who now restrains will do so until He is taken out of the way" (2 Thessalonians 2:5-7).

Something or somebody was standing in the way of the lawless man's appearance. And some of the early church fathers saw something very specific in this.

"What obstacle is there," wrote Tertullian, "but the Roman state, the falling away of which, by being scattered into ten kingdoms, shall introduce Antichrist upon (its own ruins)?" (Tertullian, *On the Resurrection of the Flesh*, chapter 24)

Building on the prophecies found in the book of Daniel, Tertullian predicted that the biggest problems for the Christian church wouldn't come from the Roman Empire itself, but from something that happened after the Empire collapsed.

For some reason, he couldn't see the man of sin becoming a problem as long as the Roman Empire stood in his way—and Paul described the man of sin appearing after a great "falling away," a time when the church itself would become unfaithful to the teachings of Christ.

When you start putting the pieces together you get a startling picture. As troublesome as the pagan Roman Empire was for the early Christian church, there were much worse problems on the horizon—distinctly *internal* problems.

As long as Rome was persecuting the church, there was little chance that the church itself could exert the kind of influence needed to produce such colossal problems. But once the Roman Empire was out of the way, the church could build on her ruins.

Which is exactly what happened. After the conversion of the Roman Emperor Constantine early in the 4th century, Christianity shifted away from its status as a despised, marginalized sect to become the official religion of the Roman Empire itself.

Then, after the empire's collapse at the hands of marauding barbarians, the church continued to expand and prosper in ways that defied imagination. Saint Augustine called the expanding Christian church "the City of God" and envisioned the church triumphing over the pagans to become a global kingdom for Christ.

But as pagan Rome gave way to a new Christian empire in the west, new problems emerged. Pagan Rome stopped persecuting Christians, but before long, Christians began to persecute each other over religious differences of opinion.

During the period known as the Dark Ages, something like 50 million people were put to death over matters of conscience. And suddenly, we see how the symbols described in the book of Revelation can be used to describe both a city *and* a church.

"I saw the woman, drunk with the blood of the saints and with the blood of the martyrs of Jesus. And when I saw her, I marveled with great amazement" (Revelation 17:6).

John is "amazed" by the sight of the woman, and given the way that John himself was persecuted by the emperor Domitian, it couldn't have been just the early Roman persecution that he witnessed. He saw an impure woman—the symbol of an unfaithful church—committing the same crimes as the Roman Emperors.

Before the consummation of history, the Bible predicts an overwhelming *religious* deception—so overwhelming that God's own people might just fall for it. And of course, that would create a situation where God's "woman"—the church—has become unfaithful.

It is interesting that, over the years, many Christians have speculated as to the identity of "Babylon" in the book of Revelation. They have said Babylon is the United States, or Russia, or a famous preacher or a well-known politician.

But God's Word is clear that in the last days, an entity that is both religious and political, an entity that embraces idol worship, an entity based in a city that sits on seven hills, an entity that has forged strong relationships with the governments of the world, an entity that has engaged in persecution for religious reasons—that is the sort of entity the Bible says will assume the role of Babylon in the last days.

The day before Thanksgiving in 1971, a man who became known as D.B. Cooper hijacked a Northwest Orient Airlines Boeing 727 traveling from Portland to Seattle. He demanded $200,000 in used $20 bills, and four parachutes.

After the other passengers had deplaned in Seattle and he had taken possession of the money and the parachutes, Cooper demanded that the plane be flown to Mexico City via Reno, where the plane would be refueled.

While en route to Reno, "Cooper" parachuted from the aircraft into a rainstorm, wearing only a business suit and light shoes. His whereabouts were never discovered. Most experts thought it was unlikely he survived his descent into the rugged, bush-covered countryside.

In 1980, a young boy vacationing with his family on the banks of the Columbia River found almost $6,000 of the ransom money given to D.B. Cooper. But although there have been numerous suspects investigated over the years, authorities are still not sure of the identity of this mystery hijacker.

Like that of D.B. Cooper, the identity of the mysterious Babylon of the book of Revelation has proven too difficult for many people to uncover.

It is curious that for hundreds of years, most of Christianity was united on the subject. History tells us that people across the centuries had a very distinct idea regarding the identity of Babylon. And that might be significant. Because history repeats. And Babylon is rising.

Special thanks to Pastor Shawn Boonstra for the content he provided for this chapter.

Chapter Six

THE WRITING ON THE WALL

In 2005, the *Economist* reported on the global boom in house prices by stating, "Never before have real house prices risen so fast, for so long, in so many countries."

The world was riding a wave of rising house prices, and because of the dramatic increase in housing values, people were flocking to invest in real estate. As several people said to me at the time, "You can't go wrong with real estate."

But the *Economist* asked a sobering question: "What if the housing boom now turns to bust?"

By now we're only too familiar with what happened. While house prices rose an average of a staggering 73% between 1997 and 2005, by 2011, houses in Detroit, Cleveland and Las Vegas were costing less than they did in January 2000. Numerous other housing markets in the United States are experiencing similar declines. As has frequently been said, what goes up must come down.

The great kingdoms that have appeared on the world stage have without exception passed from prominence after a period of time. Monuments in the Middle Eastern sands silently testify that Egypt was once a dominant political and military power.

Such was its power that few living 2,000 years ago would ever have thought that the mighty Roman Empire would ever come to an end. Covering around 2 million square miles and stretching across Europe from the Scottish border to the edge of what are now Pakistan and Afghanistan, it seemed as if the Roman Empire could never know defeat.

In more modern times, what was once the Soviet Union is now a collection of independent states, none of which come close to matching the might of the former USSR.

The book of Revelation says that "last-days Babylon" will dominate planet Earth economically, socially and spiritually—its power in the world entirely unprecedented. Dissenters against her authority will be punished ruthlessly, and a death sentence ultimately pronounced against all who refuse to yield to her governance (Revelation 13).

But according to the Bible, "Babylon the great", the one who "saith in her heart, I sit a queen, and am no widow, and shall see no sorrow" (Revelation 18:7), will ultimately be brought to naught, receiving "the cup of the wine of the fierceness of [God's] wrath" (Revelation 16:19).

Prophecy's sentence is, "Babylon is fallen" (Revelation 14:8).

What precipitates the demise of the dominant global power at the end of the age? How can Babylon experience such a dramatic fall after having exerted control over "the kings of the earth" and "the merchants of the earth"? (Revelation 18:3)

The fall of ancient Babylon helps us understand the decline and fall of modern Babylon in the book of Revelation. Babylon ruled the ancient world from around 605 BC to 539 BC, during which time she amassed such fortune and power as to be referred to as "the praise of the whole earth" (Jeremiah 51:41).

Though it was definitely a power that caused tremendous suffering to God's people, through His dealings with ancient Babylon, God was seeking to save Babylon's inhabitants and turn their hearts toward Him.

God's purposes are always redemptive. It is recorded in the Bible that the great Babylonian King Nebuchadnezzar converted from paganism to faith in God, having witnessed God's providence and leading and having had a personal encounter with God that left Him convinced of God's goodness (Daniel 4:34-37).

But the Bible records that ultimately, Babylon refused to surrender to the guidance of God's Holy Spirit. "We would have healed Babylon," God said, "but she is not healed" (Jeremiah 51:9). Here's what happened.

In the year 539 BC, Nebuchadnezzar's grandson, Belshazzar, was co-regent in Babylon along with his father, Nabonidus. At a time when Nabonidus had left Babylon to worship the moon god, Sin, in another part of the kingdom, Babylon came under attack by the armies of Medo-Persia.

This invasion had many years before been predicted by the prophet Isaiah. "Thus saith the Lord to his anointed," Isaiah wrote, "to Cyrus, whose right hand I have holden, to subdue nations before him; and I will loose the two leaved gates; and the gates shall not be shut" (Isaiah 45:1).

The armies of Medo-Persia diverted the Euphrates River—which ran through the city of Babylon—from its course. They then marched in shallow water, or along the dry riverbed, right through the "two leaved gates" that had been carelessly left open, exposing Babylon to attack and ultimate defeat.

On the night Babylon was conquered by the Medo-Persians, Belshazzar "made a great feast to a thousand of his lords, and drank wine before the thousand" (Daniel 5:1).

Engrossed in debauchery and careless about the security of the city, Belshazzar, in a rash, alcohol-fueled episode of blasphemy, "commanded to bring the golden and silver vessels which his father Nebuchadnezzaar had taken out of the temple which was in Jerusalem; that the king, his princes, his wives and his concubines, might drink therein" (Daniel 5:2).

The gravity of this situation must not be overlooked. Years before, Nebuchadnezzar's armies, when sacking Jerusalem, plundered the temple and made off with the sacred vessels used in the worship of God. Nebuchadnezzar recognized something of the sanctity of these items, having them placed in "the treasure house of his god" (Daniel 1:2).

These vessels were *exceedingly* sacred, having been used in the Jewish temple services. And now, Belshazzar, the ruler in Babylon, was bringing out worship vessels sacred to the

God of Heaven, that with them he might pay homage to heathen gods.

"They drank wine, and praised the gods of gold, and of silver, of brass, of iron, or wood, and of stone" (Daniel 5:4).

Belshazzar took what was holy to God—dedicated to the true worship of the true God—and used those holy things in praise of pagan deities. When he did so, the God of Heaven decreed that Belshazzar had crossed the line of rebellion.

An invisible hand appeared from out of the sleeve of darkness, and, quite literally, the writing was on the wall for not only Belshazzar, but for the kingdom of Babylon.

"In the same hour came forth fingers of a man's hand, and wrote over against the candlestick upon the plaster of the wall of the king's palace" (Daniel 5:5).

Belshazzar was terrified by what he saw happening before his eyes, recognizing even in his drunken stupor that something supernatural was taking place.

Eventually, the prophet Daniel was summoned to interpret the mysterious writing for the king, but before doing so, he explained to Belshazzar why this moment had come. He recounted God's dealings with Belshazzar's grandfather, Nebuchadnezzar, reminding Belshazzar that as great as Nebuchadnezzar was, he governed only due to the providence of God.

Daniel then recalled for the intoxicated monarch how, due to his pride, Nebuchadnezzar "was deposed from his kingly throne" and afflicted with a temporary insanity, living in the wilderness like a wild animal.

"And thou his son, O Belshazzar, hast not humbled thine heart, though thou knewest all this; but hast lifted up thyself against the Lord of heaven; and they have brought the vessels of his house before thee, and thou, and thy lords... have drunk wine in them; and thou hast praised the gods of silver and gold..." (Daniel 5:22-23)

According to Daniel, Belshazzar knew about God's dealing with his grandfather. Belshazzar knew the kingdom was entrusted to him by God, and that the worship vessels he brought out to liven up his party were the holy property of a holy God.

Fully cognizant that he was in rebellion against Heaven, Belshazzar pressed on in his orgy of indulgence.

Then Daniel interpreted the writing on the wall in three statements. The first stated, "God hath numbered thy kingdom, and finished it."

The second mysterious phrase was decoded to mean, "Thou art weighed in the balances, and are found wanting."

And finally, God's message to Belshazzar was, "Thy kingdom is divided, and given to the Medes and Persians."

"In that night was Belshazzar the king of the Chaldeans slain. And Darius the Median took the kingdom, being about threescore and two years old" (Daniel 5:30-31).

Babylon had fallen.

In the same way, the Bible makes clear that Babylon will fall again, when in God's final Gospel message to the world, an angel flying in the mist of heaven announces that "Babylon is fallen" (Revelation 14:8).

What is it that precipitates the fall of modern Babylon? Remember, ancient Babylon ultimately fell when the ruler of the kingdom took objects designed to be used in true worship and completely desecrated them by employing them in pagan worship practices. God's Law was set aside, and true worship was rejected in favor of false, pagan worship.

If we apply the Bible rule of type and antitype, we can expect that in the book of Revelation, we would have a world-ruling power corrupting that which God has intended to be used in true worship, and replacing it instead with false worship. Does this scenario play out in the book of Revelation?

Throughout Bible history, we see that a jealous fallen angel has built his appeal to the human family around the issue of worship. In an attempt to receive the glory and honor due only to God, Satan has endeavored to draw people to worship *him* rather than worship God.

It is easy to see how he has accomplished this through pagan and New Age religious practices—few would argue that people worshiping the earth or worshiping idols or offering sacrifices to appease evil spirits are engaged in worship of the true God of Heaven.

But how would Satan deceive *Christian* people? How would he get people off-target spiritually while these people carried Bibles and regularly attended church?

In the first half of Revelation chapter 13, we read that not only will "all the world" wonder "after the beast," but the vast majority will worship the dragon (Satan) and worship the beast.

God's true worshipers will, as Jesus said, "worship Him in Spirit and in truth" (John 4:24), while Babylon's followers will worship God in vain, "teaching for doctrines the commandments of men" (Matthew 15:9).

God's Law is set aside and human laws are exalted in their place, something God is unable to tolerate for long. As David wrote in the Psalms, "It is time for thee, Lord, to work: for they have made void thy law" (Psalm 119:126).

Just as Belshazzar understood the seriousness of taking that which is holy to God and using it in false worship, everyone living on planet Earth in history's final days will hear God's call in the everlasting Gospel to "worship Him who made heaven, and earth, and the sea, and the fountains of waters" (Revelation 14:7).

God's last message to the world contains an appeal to worship God consistent with the Bible's guidelines for true worship. The message is presented as though being proclaimed by an "angel flying in the mist of heaven" speaking with a "loud voice" to "every nation, kindred, tongue and people" (Revelation 14:6).

The whole world will hear God's appeal to faithfulness and obedience. And once the issues in Earth's final conflict have been presented to the inhabitants of Earth, and people everywhere have been given an opportunity to decide for or against the truth of God's Word, then it will be said that "Babylon is fallen."

Which is itself a message that demonstrates God's great love for the world. Remember, the word "Babylon" means "confusion". That there is a Babylon in the last days implies that there is mass spiritual confusion in the world. And this confusion was instigated and cultivated over millennia by an angry devil who is bound and determined to receive on Earth the worship he was unsuccessful in receiving in Heaven.

One might expect that God would have little time for anyone who is confused or deceived or spiritually misled. However, instead of impatiently cutting off the erring, God appeals with a message designed to jar people into spiritual consciousness and draw them to faith in Him. Virtually an entire global population is led astray by the enemy of souls, yet God calls to all the world with a message of repentance.

So if all the world "wondered after the beast", and if the beast—Babylon—falls, what is the fate of the people who have chosen to follow Babylon? What hope is there for a person trying to make their way though this world and into the world to come? The good news is: God has that all figured out. Which is a good thing for us today. Because Babylon is rising.

Chapter Seven

THE FINAL CALL

Legend has it that after a decade of unsuccessfully attempting to overthrow the city of Troy, the Greek military decided to change its strategy, and rather than using force to overthrow the Trojans, they resorted to treachery.

They constructed a large, wooden horse, and left it—and 30 or so soldiers hidden inside—outside the gates of Troy. After the Greeks pretended to sail away from the city, the Trojans brought the giant horse inside their city, believing the horse would bring them blessings and power.

The hidden soldiers were then released from their wooden horse by a sympathetic spy. They opened the gates of the city, and the Greek army—having returned under cover of darkness—entered Troy and vanquished their enemy.

The Greeks were victorious because of the Trojan Horse. To the people of Troy, it appeared attractive and desirable, but ultimately brought about the ruin of their city.

In the same way, Satan employs a Trojan horse in the final days of the history of the world—in a determined attempt to strike against the heart of God and His Kingdom.

Seeking to turn humanity away from loyalty to the Creator, he ultimately presents to the world the enormous deception of the mark of the beast. With Jesus' return imminent, Satan introduces a deception calculated to lead men and women away from fidelity to God—knowing from experience that unfaithfulness to God in Earth's final hours can only bring spiritual ruin.

In Revelation chapter 18, God speaks in no uncertain terms regarding Babylon. A messenger from Heaven cries "mightily with a strong voice, saying, Babylon the great is fallen, is fallen, and is become the habitation of devils, and the hold of every foul spirit, and a cage of every unclean and hateful bird" (Revelation 18:2).

God's assessment of Babylon cannot be misinterpreted: Babylon has opposed the truth of God, confused people with false doctrines and deceptive teachings, and led people away from obedience to God's Law. Babylon is fallen.

"For all nations have drunk of the wine of the wrath of her fornication, and the kings of the earth have committed fornication with her, and the merchants of the earth are waxed rich through the abundance of her delicacies" (Revelation 18:3).

Not only has Babylon been spiritually unfaithful, but she has been involved in illicit alliances with the nations of the earth, enriching many by her favors and influence.

Then God issues a final call to His remaining faithful ones still connected with Babylon. In Revelation 18:4, the Bible says, "And I heard another voice from heaven, saying, Come out of her, my people, that ye be not partakers of her sins, and that ye receive not of her plagues."

God maintains His redemptive demeanor until the very end of human history, appealing to all who are following Babylon to cut their ties with Babylon and boldly stand on God's side in the battle between truth and error, between light and dark—and ultimately, between Christ and Satan.

The urgency of God's call to faithfulness is tremendous. Those who remain connected to the spiritual falsehood and apostasy of Babylon will "receive of her plagues" (Revelation 18:4).

These are the seven last plagues described in Revelation 16 as the wrath of God is poured out on a disobedient world just prior to Jesus' return.

Revelation 14:10 says that those who receive the mark of the beast—a mark of loyalty to Babylon and of disloyalty to God—will drink the "wine of the wrath of God", described as the "seven last plagues" in Revelation 15:1. The plagues are visited upon Babylon and all who choose to stand allied with her.

The first plagues is a "foul and loathsome sore" (Revelation 16:2) that afflicts those who "had the mark of the beast...and them which worshiped his image."

The second plague sees the oceans of the earth become like the blood of a dead man, while the third plague sees the "rivers and fountains of waters" become blood (Revelation 16:3, 4).

Sea creatures will die, ocean-going vessels will not be able to traverse the seas, supplies of fresh drinking water will be seriously affected and the effect on the environment will be cataclysmic.

Keep in mind that Babylon tells the world that if the mark of the beast is received, safety and financial security are assured. Those who take the mark of the beast are told that if they do so they will be able to buy and sell (Revelation 13:17).

They are told that they will avoid physical punishment (Revelation 13:15). Yet the seven last plagues reveal that Babylon cannot provide the security and protection it has promised the world. Babylon is revealed as a pretender.

The fourth plague sees the sun scorch people with intense heat (Revelation 16:8), while the fifth plague brings intense darkness to the Earth.

It isn't difficult to see the similarities between these seven last plagues and the plagues that fell in Egypt in the days of Moses. Of the 10 plagues that fell in the time of Moses, the first three affected both God's people and the enemies of God, while the seven last plagues afflicted only the Egyptians.

Here is Heaven's assurance that the plagues in the last days will affect only the enemies of God, while God's people—as in ancient Egypt—will be divinely protected.

The seven last plagues continue with the battle of Armageddon and a final plague that brings about the complete annihilation of Babylon. The largest earthquake in the history of the world causes islands to sink and mountains to crumble, while hailstones weighing as much as 70 pounds or more crash to the ground with intense ferocity, devastating the Earth.

"And great Babylon was remembered before God, to give her the cup of the wine of the fierceness of His wrath" (Revelation 16:19).

Babylon is finally destroyed, and those who allied themselves with Babylon and rejected the sovereignty of God in their lives find that they are eternally outside the mercy of God.

The seven last plagues demonstrate to the universe that the only safe path for God's children is to cling by faith to God under any circumstances. The plagues also reveal that to accept a change in God's Word and to choose the authority of a created being over that of the Creator—essentially, to repeat Satan's original misdeed in Heaven—is disastrous.

For thousands of years, God has appealed to people to trust Him, to include Him in their lives on an intimate basis, and to make His will the foundation of their lives. God knows that His Word and His will are the only paths of true safety for the believer. Jesus said, "I am the way, the truth and the life" (John 14:6).

His words were a simple statement of fact: we're only safe from Satan's deceptions if we cling to Jesus. Speaking of Satan, Jesus said, "The thief cometh not, but for to steal, and to kill, and to destroy..." (John 10:10)

But God describes His Law as a hedge of protection (James 2:12) and His Word as the guide for our lives (Psalm 119:105).

Isaiah wrote of God's solicitude for His people when He said, "What could have been done more to my vineyard, that I have not done in it?" (Isaiah 5:4)

God has done all He can to convince the world that His thoughts toward humanity are "thoughts of peace and not of evil" (Jeremiah 29:11).

Tragically, the great majority of people will finally choose to reject God's invitation of mercy and His gift of everlasting life. In Earth's final days, in a virtual repeat of what happened 2,000 years ago, Jesus comes unto His own, and His own receive Him not.

Throughout the Bible, God's dealings with the human family have been consistent. Let's keep in mind that it was humanity's own choice to go it alone and forfeit God's blessing. In the Garden of Eden, Adam and Eve ate the forbidden fruit with full knowledge of what would result. "In the day thou eatest thereof, thou shalt surely die" (Genesis 2:17).

But when Adam and Eve chose sin over obedience, what was God's reaction? God pursued the insubordinate couple, and although He was forced to banish them from the Garden of Eden, He forgave their sin and held out to them forgiveness at what would be an enormous cost to Himself.

The Godhead chose that Jesus would die in the place of sinful human beings, in what would be not only a demonstration of mercy, but would also reveal to the world what God's character is truly like.

Jesus said, "Come to me...and I will give you rest" (Matthew 11:28).

But in John 5:40, He said, "Ye will not come to me, that ye might have life."

Tragically, the devil has provoked people into believing that life is more fulfilling when they go their own way independent of God. The seven last plagues reveal—finally and forever—that the path of life is the path Jesus walked before us, that of closeness to God and complete surrender to Him.

Throughout history, rebellion against God has always resulted in heartache and hardship. Upon their eviction from Eden, the lives of Adam and Eve immediately became lives of hardship and sorrow.

Israel's lack of faith in God led them to spend 40 additional years in the wilderness. Israel's stubborn disobedience led them into captivity in ancient Babylon. Instead of welcoming the Messiah when He appeared in their midst, Christ's people consigned Him to an agonizing death on the cross, and suffered in the aftermath of that decision.

In excluding God from one's life, a person elects to forsake much of the blessing of the God of Heaven, with sin ultimately causing separation from God (Isaiah 59:2).

Throughout the entire history of the cosmos, God has been trying to persuade men and women that He is love. The first great rebel, however, has spent thousands of years trying to convince the human family that God is harsh and tyrannical.

God stands guilty of working to draw people to Him so they might experience the joy of everlasting life in a world no longer infected with the disease of sin.

Satan, the accuser of God's people (Revelation 12:10), maligns the character of God. Tragically, masses of people today choose to side with Satan and array themselves against the Source of love and life.

There is a real spiritual battle going on right now on planet Earth, as real as any war that has ever taken place. From the day Satan rebelled in Heaven, he has been trying to drag people down to the place where they cannot be saved. He knows how precious they are in the sight of God.

He knows that "God is not willing that any should perish, but that all should come to repentance" (2 Peter 3:9).

Better than anyone, Satan knows that "God so loved the world, that He gave His only begotten Son, that whosoever believeth in Him should not perish, but have everlasting life" (John 3:16).

Awestruck by the great love of God for the human family, the Apostle John wrote in 1 John 3:1, "Behold, what manner of love the Father hath bestowed upon us, that we should be called the sons of God..."

Today, the enemy of souls portrays Christians as being ignorant and out of touch. Those who believe the Creation account in Scripture are backward thinkers who are out of step with science. Those who oppose modern liberalization of moral standards are intolerant, while those who believe in obeying God are depicted as legalistic.

Satan has worked intentionally over the passing years, marginalizing Christians, denigrating the divine, and elevating human wisdom and a do-as-you-please attitude that makes humans into gods and God into a mockery.

Concealing his strategy in skepticism, intellectualism and materialism, he appeals to the world with a definite purpose: to lead people to live their lives without the Word of God as the basis for their decisions. The results of such a decision are staggeringly tragic: people lost for eternity, and separated from the One who is life.

The seven last plagues are soon to be poured out on an unsuspecting planet. And Satan rejoices. He sees men and women being manipulated by the forces of darkness to choose death over life, and to reject the authority of God in their lives. As they do so, there is something Satan knows better than anyone: Babylon is rising.

Chapter Eight

HISTORY'S GREATEST EVENT

A number of years ago, I decided to read a book that had been hanging around the family bookshelves for some years. With a few days to fill, I set about reading the story of an Englishman who had been falsely accused of a crime, unjustly convicted and sent to live out his life in the penal colony of Australia.

The book graphically portrayed the brutal realities of prison life, and the hero of the story suffered incredible cruelty. As I recall, he somehow discovered he had an inheritance back in England, but to return to England was—for him—an impossibility.

Predictably, he falls for a lovely young lady, and then, remarkably, they both manage to escape and board a ship that would take them away to freedom together.

Just as I was rejoicing that the 400-plus pages I had read were finally going to add up to something happy, the boat in which our liberated couple was sailing met a storm and...sank. The hero and his lady friend both drowned. And that was that.

Owing to its setting and content, reading the book had been hard work, but I pressed ahead stoically because I was sure the book would conclude with a happy ending. But it did not.

The poor, falsely-accused man was shipped halfway around the planet, suffered every imaginable indignity at the hands of his brutal captors, finally made a dash for freedom, and died in the process. What an ending. And from my point of view as a reader, what a terrible ending!

I'm thankful the Bible has a happy ending. The Bible starts out wonderfully: "In the beginning God created the heaven and the earth" (Genesis 1:1). The stars are hung in the sky, the planet is clothed with beauty, the animals are brought forth and Adam and Eve are created.

But it doesn't take long for everything to take a turn for the worse. Sin entered the world and brought with it the curse of death. The entire human family rebelled against God. God graciously promised that Jesus would come to the world (Genesis 3:15), but precious few people responded with favor to God's wonderful pledge.

Only eight people could be found to save on Noah's ark, and they were hardly the purest people to have ever lived. Believers in God were in the minority. When Jesus came to the world, He only had 12 disciples, and one of them betrayed Him to be murdered.

The early Christian church was confronted with a Herculean task. Eleven men commissioned by Jesus to "teach all nations" were pitted against an unbelieving world and the malignant wrath of Satan and his demons. A person reading the Bible for the first time might almost expect things to turn out for the church like they did for the poor fugitive who fled from the penal colony.

But the Bible is a book with a happy ending. The final chapter of the Bible pictures the redeemed in Heaven with Jesus, emancipated from the tyranny of sin.

The Bible says, "And there shall be no more curse" (Revelation 22:3).

Sin is gone forever. Satan no longer tempts God's people and causes misery and woe. Babylon no longer exists, and God's people "shall reign for ever and ever" (Revelation 22:5).

God's intention at Creation was that all people be happy and holy, and enjoy His blessing for as long as time lasted. But God took a risk in that He created human beings with the freedom of choice: there existed the possibility that people would squander their freedom of choice and opt to live for themselves rather than for the glory of their Maker.

Satan made that very decision in Heaven, and upon coming to the Earth tempted our original grandparents to do the same thing. And when they did—disobeying God and choosing self-will instead of God's will—the result was sin, which the Bible says leads to death (Romans 6:23). Adam and Eve had forfeited union with the Source of life. They had to die.

But as someone once said, as soon as there was sin, there was a Savior. The Bible describes Jesus as the "Lamb slain from the foundation of the world" (Revelation 13:8).

From the time God made the promise to Adam and Eve that a Savior would come, people have been looking forward to the greatest event in the history of time—the return of Jesus Christ.

Jesus came once to the world as a baby in a manger, born to live among men and die a brutal death on a Roman instrument of torture. His mission was not only to die for the sins of fallen human beings, but—more importantly—to reveal to the human family what God is really like. As Jesus once said to his disciples, "he that hath seen me hath seen the Father" (John 14:9).

Jesus came to the world to reveal the character of God to the universe. Millennia ago, Satan convinced one-third of the angels in heaven to choose exile from Heaven rather than yield to God's leadership (Revelation 12:4).

Satan convinced Eve that God was keeping blessings from her when he lied to her in the Garden of Eden (Genesis 3:5). And from that time to this, he has worked to convince people that they are better off without God in their lives and should live without reference to Him.

All God has ever wanted to do is bless people as much as possible. In response to humanity's fall into sin, God's purpose has been to lift up and restore. Even the worst sinners are offered God's pardon. Jesus said, "him that cometh to me I will in no wise cast out" (John 6:37).

And to all who choose Jesus as their Savior, God promises the greatest event in the history of the cosmos. One day soon, Jesus is going to return to this Earth.

And when He does, "the dead in Christ shall rise" (1 Thessalonians 4:16), and those among the living who have allowed Him fully into their lives "shall be caught up together with them in the clouds to meet the Lord in the air" (1 Thessalonians 4:17). And all of the redeemed shall "be with the Lord" forever.

No wonder Paul referred to the return of Jesus as the "blessed hope" (Titus 2:13). When Jesus returns, sin will have come to an end, sickness will be gone forever, and there will be no more sadness, no more tragedy, no more separation, and no more death. As Jesus says in Revelation 21:5, "Behold, I make all things new."

There are only two paths a person can follow in this world: that of seeking God and His will for one's life, or the path of self-interest. Really, it's that simple. We're either seeking God's will or we're seeking our own. And only one of those paths leads to everlasting life.

The fact is, everyone alive is in need of the mercy of God. Paul wrote that "all have sinned, and come short of the glory of God" (Romans 3:23).

That's me, you, your neighbors, your friends... everyone. And as the wages of sin is death (Romans 6:23), the outlook for the human family is bleak. Unless...

Unless we choose Jesus. Jesus offers us life in place of death, by forgiving our sins and giving us new hearts and minds. God has said, "If we confess our sins, He is faithful and just to forgive us our sins and to cleanse us from all unrighteousness" (1 John 1:9).

It isn't that we confess our sins in order to inform God of something He didn't know already. Confession helps us see the destructive nature of sin and the exalted nature of God.

Once we have confessed our sins, we claim Christ as our hope and believe in God's ability to save us. As Paul told a hardened jail keeper one night, "Believe on the Lord Jesus Christ, and thou shalt be saved" (Acts 16:31).

When you believe God has forgiven you, cleansed you and made you His own, you can have the assurance that, as Paul told the church at Corinth, "old things are passed away: behold, all things are become new" (2 Corinthians 5:17).

And then? Then you live your life in connection with God, following His leading and making His Word the basis for your existence. As Jesus said, "Seek ye first the kingdom of God, and His righteousness" (Matthew 6:33).

And while life will bring its ups and downs, you can live with the assurance that God is with you, and that the best is yet to come!

When my daughter was eight years old, she said to me out of the blue, "Daddy, I'm glad I'm not an atheist!"

Well, I was glad about that too, but I was interested to know what lay behind her thinking. "Why's that sweetheart?" I asked.

"Because if I was an atheist, who would I be able to turn to when things get rough? I'd have to rely on myself, and I don't think that's a good idea."

I had to agree. Who does a person turn to when things get rough? What does a person have who does not have Jesus in their life? I'm not suggesting a non-Christian cannot be happy in this world. There are many people alive who are apparently doing perfectly well facing life without the help of God.

But what happens when things get rough? A lady I spoke with just days ago told me she was about to have breast cancer surgery. Her husband of 50+ years had recently died, and her mother had passed away a short time after. But she told me she could face the surgery with confidence because she knew she could lean on God.

Which is not to say the surgery will save her life. After all, death awaits us all. But what does a person have who gets to the end of his or her life without hope in God? What lies beyond that person's final breath?

For the Christian, there is the hope—the certainty—of the return of Jesus. The dead in Christ will live again, and living believers will be translated to live forever in a remade world.

But what if you don't have that hope, friend? Could you be satisfied to live in this world, and shun the world to come?

But even more importantly, what about Jesus' death for you? Would you really feel good knowing Someone had died for you—willingly given His life for you—and you had just gone on as though you didn't care?

There are few people today who don't respond tenderly to simple kindnesses and casual courtesies. But just think a moment: Someone died for you. The eternal Son of God poured Himself into human flesh so that He could live in this world and die for your sins. If you think about that a moment, it has to mean something to you.

A lot of people today have dismissed faith, dismissed the Bible, and dismissed the whole notion of God simply because our society isn't geared toward faith in God. We live in a skeptical world, where reason and science often trump faith and trust.

The master conspirator has been working to this end for millennia. But if you were to take a moment and investigate the Bible, there's a very good chance you would say to yourself, "Maybe there's something to this. Maybe my life would be bettered by faith in God. Maybe if I let Jesus into my life, He could really help me..."

The Second Coming of Jesus is getting closer every day. The Bible says that in that glorious moment, the heavens will depart like a scroll (Revelation 6:14), and Jesus and the angels of Heaven will approach the Earth to finally ransom those who have been faithful to God, even amidst the tremendous difficulties of Earth's final days.

Those who have not chosen Jesus will realize—too late—that they have lost everything (Revelation 6:14-17), while those who exercised simple faith in God and accepted forgiveness for sin will gain a life that measures with the life of God (Revelation 21:3, 4).

How is it with you? How are things between you and God today? Jesus made an incredible offer when He said in Isaiah 27:5, "Let him take hold of my strength, that he may make peace with me; and he shall make peace with me."

Is there anything preventing you from taking hold of God and making peace with Him today? Only one thing can ever stand between a person and God, and that is an individual's choice. Will you choose God, salvation and eternity today?

When my son was two years old, I decided it would be fun if we enjoyed the best breakfast a couple of men could pull together.

"Let's go, Son! We're off to the supermarket to buy anything you want for breakfast tomorrow. We're going to have the best breakfast ever!"

Jacob needed no coaxing. He was into his car seat like a flash, and before long we were walking the aisles of our local Food Lion, looking for all his favorite foods. (In the interest of full disclosure, I should probably point out that at two years of age, his list of favorite foods was not very long).

We headed to the fruits and vegetables section.

"Son! Bananas!"

Yes, Jacob liked the look of the long, yellow bananas, and agreed we should have some of them for breakfast the next day.

We grabbed some pears, some peaches, and I even chose to ignore the price of the watermelons to ensure a happy breakfast for my little boy (and his watermelon-loving father).

"Apples, Daddy!" Jacob said, spying a display of gorgeous pink apples.

"Oh, son!" I exclaimed. "These aren't just apples—they're New Zealand apples!"

Jacob was ecstatic. Even though he was only two years old, he knew well that New Zealand apples are the best apples money can buy.

We arrived home anticipating a breakfast fit for a king. We washed some items, refrigerated others, picked some blueberries from the bushes in our backyard, and waited for morning to come.

When it did, I bounded down the stairs to prepare the meal for what was then our family of three. Imagine my surprise, then, when I saw that my son was already eating. Eating noodles. Eating noodles out of the trash!

"Jacob! What are you doing?" I gasped.

Jacob was delighted. "Noonles, Daddy. Noonles!" he said, holding up a "noonle" so I could see what he was enjoying so enthusiastically.

"I can see they're noonles, Son, but what are you doing eating out of the trash? That's dirty! And Son," I said with a hint of dismay in my voice, "have you forgotten what Daddy has for you? Look," I said, as I opened the fridge. "Watermelon! Cantaloupe! Blueberries! Apples!"

"New Zealand apples, Daddy!" Jacob corrected me, now smiling big and climbing into his chair.

Breakfast really was good that morning, but my son would have been quite content to miss it all and eat out of the trash instead.

That made me think. How often do people forget all about the feast prepared for them by their Father, and eat the garbage of the world instead?

Could it be that God has blessings for you that you've ignored? Could it be that you've limped along on little when you could have been soaring on much?

The greatest event in history is soon to take place, and Jesus wants very much for you to be ready to meet Him when He comes again. A person can only gain by choosing Jesus. The spiritual battle we're involved in is very, very real. And time to choose for Christ is running out.

Because Babylon is rising.

NOTES

NOTES